THE SCIENCE BEHIND
NATURAL PHENOMENA

THE SCIENCE BEHIND

WONDERS OF THE
SUN

SUN DOGS, LUNAR ECLIPSES, AND GREEN FLASH

BY SUZANNE GARBE

CONSULTANT:
DR. KAREN SCHWARZ
ASSOCIATE PROFESSOR, DEPARTMENT OF GEOLOGY AND ASTRONOMY,
WEST CHESTER UNIVERSITY, WEST CHESTER, PENNSYLVANIA

CAPSTONE PRESS
a capstone imprint

Edge Books are published by Capstone Press,
1710 Roe Crest Drive, North Mankato, Minnesota 56003
www.mycapstone.com

Library of Congress Cataloging-in-Publication Data
Names: Garbe, Suzanne, author.
Title: The science behind wonders of the sun : sun dogs, lunar eclipses, and
green flash / by Suzanne Garbe.
Description: North Mankato, Minnesota : Capstone Press, [2017] | Series: Edge
books. The science behind natural phenomena | Audience: Ages 9–15. |
Audience: Grades 4 to 6. | Includes bibliographical references and index.
Identifiers: LCCN 2016005492| ISBN 9781515707783 (library binding) | ISBN
9781515707837 (paperback) | ISBN 9781515707882 (ebook (pdf))
Subjects: LCSH: Solar-terrestrial physics—Juvenile literature. | Solar
activity—Juvenile literature. | Sun—Miscellanea—Juvenile literature.
Classification: LCC QB539.T4 G37 2017 | DDC 523.7/2—dc23
LC record available at http://lccn.loc.gov/2016005492

Editorial Credits
Linda Staniford, editor; Terri Poburka, designer;
Svetlana Zhurkin, media researcher; Laura Manthe, production specialist

Photo Credits
iStockphoto: skhoward, 26; NASA, 7, 17; NASA, ESA, and the Hubble Heritage, 5;
Newscom: Kyodo, 23, 24 (top); Shutterstock: 3DMAVR, 6, andras_csontos, 25, Andrey
Armyagov, 21, Astrobobo, 10, 12 (top), Danshutter, 11 (left), Karin Hildebrand Lau, 29,
LagunaticPhoto, 12–13, Naeblys, 14–15, Peter Hermes Furian, 24 (bottom), seveniwe,
16, underworld, 4–5, VikaSuh, 1 and throughout, Vitaly Titov, 27; SOHO (ESA &
NASA), cover, 8, 19, 20; Svetlana Zhurkin, 11 (right)

Printed and bound in the United States of America.
001105

TABLE OF
CONTENTS

OUR SPECIAL SUN

Many pieces of art, including comics and cartoons, picture the Sun as a solid yellow circle. That's how most of us imagine the Sun.

However, scientists are able to study the Sun closely using special **telescopes** and other instruments. They see much more than the yellow circle most of us imagine. They see and study **phenomena** such as sunspots, solar flares, and lunar eclipses.

To **astronomers**, the Sun isn't that special. Our Sun is simply one of many stars in the universe. There may be as many as 100 billion stars in our galaxy alone!

Yet the Sun is vital to human life. Without it, Earth would be cold and dark. Plants wouldn't grow. Humans couldn't live. Because the Sun is so important to us, many astronomers are interested in studying it. What they've learned about the Sun is fascinating.

A solar telescope in Tenerife, Spain, helps astronomers learn ⟶ *about the Sun.*

Life Cycle of the Sun

All stars follow a similar life cycle. Most stars begin with a huge cloud of hydrogen gas that gravity pulls together. Over time, the hydrogen is slowly burned off. This is what makes stars give off heat and light. This can take millions or billions of years.

Our Sun is about 4.5 to 5 billion years old. Scientists think it will burn for at least 5 billion more years before it runs out of hydrogen.

Stars are formed in clouds of gas.

telescope—an instrument made of lenses and mirrors that is used to view distant objects

phenomena—very unusual or remarkable events

astronomer—a scientist who studies stars, planets, and other objects in space

SUNSPOTS

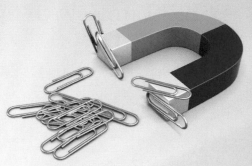

One of the first discoveries scientists made about the Sun was that it has dark spots. Scientists first observed these sunspots in the 1600s. Sunspots are areas of the Sun that are cooler, and therefore less bright, than the rest of the Sun.

To understand sunspots, you have to first understand magnetic fields. A magnetic field is the area around an object where magnetism is in effect. Magnetic fields can cause other objects to be pulled in or pushed away. Imagine a magnet sitting on a desk. Now imagine bringing a paper clip closer and closer to the magnet. When the paper clip starts to be pulled toward the magnet, it has entered the magnetic field.

The Sun, Earth, and many other stars and planets are filled with **particles** that have a magnetic charge. As a result, these stars and planets are surrounded by magnetic fields. The Sun's magnetic field changes the way hot gases in the Sun move. This leads to the Sun having some cooler areas, which we call sunspots.

AMAZING FACT

Sunspots are only 25 percent as bright as the rest of the Sun. However, even when there are spots on the sun, it is still bright enough to damage your eyes permanently if you look directly at it. And we are 93 million miles (150 million kilometers) away!

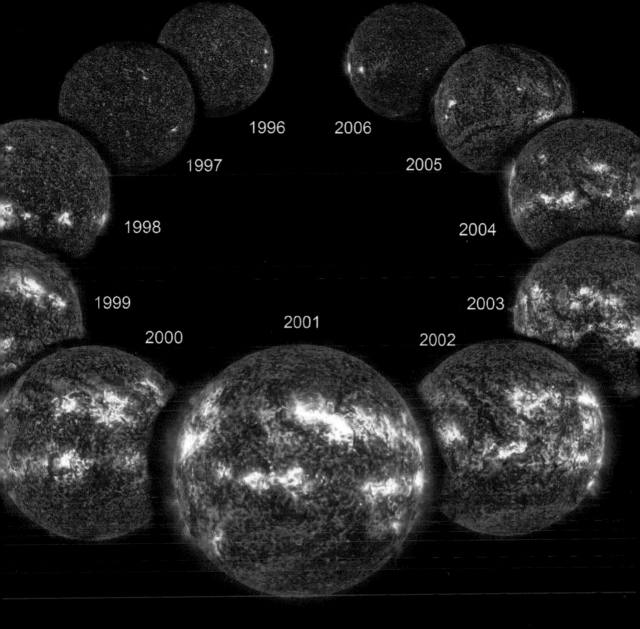

1996 2006
1997 2005
1998 2004
1999 2003
2000 2001 2002

This image shows the solar cycle. In this image the sunspots are the lighter patches. The number of sunspots on the surface of the Sun changes every 11 years.

particle—a very tiny piece of an object

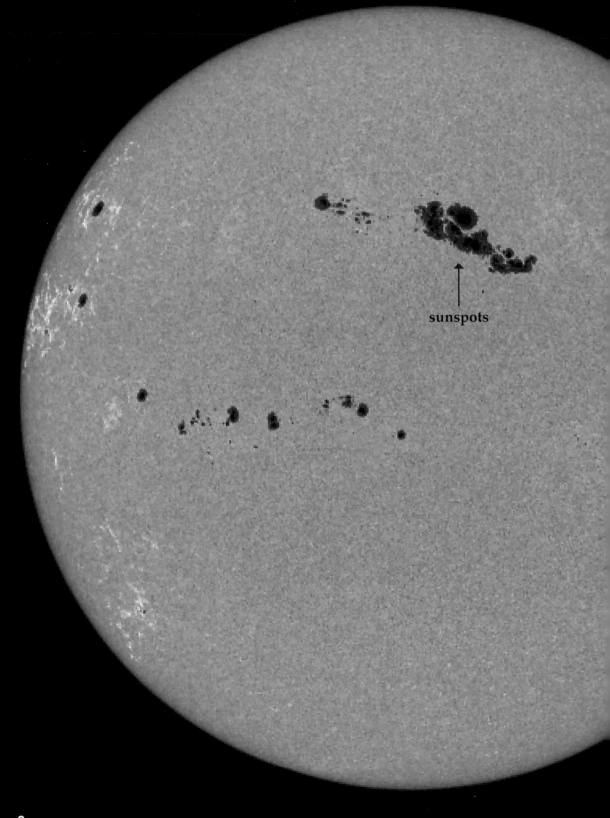

sunspots

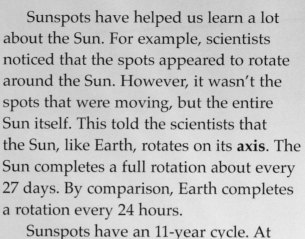

Sunspots have helped us learn a lot about the Sun. For example, scientists noticed that the spots appeared to rotate around the Sun. However, it wasn't the spots that were moving, but the entire Sun itself. This told the scientists that the Sun, like Earth, rotates on its **axis**. The Sun completes a full rotation about every 27 days. By comparison, Earth completes a rotation every 24 hours.

Sunspots have an 11-year cycle. At the start of the cycle, the Sun has very few spots. Over the next five years, more and more sunspots will occur. Then the number of sunspots falls again. Sunspot locations also move during this cycle. Over time they move toward and then away from the equator. This 11-year pattern is called the sunspot cycle. It is part of the larger **solar** cycle.

Each individual sunspot also has times of growth and decline. Each sunspot starts small, gets larger, and then shrinks to nothing. A sunspot can last anywhere from a few hours to several months. More than half of all sunspots last for 48 hours or less.

axis—an imaginary line around which something rotates
solar—having to do with the Sun

SOLAR AND LUNAR ECLIPSES

If the moon passes between the Sun and Earth, it can block the Sun's light. When this happens it's called a solar **eclipse**. Solar eclipses usually happen just once or twice a year. They are visible only from a few parts of Earth, and they last for just a few minutes.

There are several types of solar eclipses. One reason for this is that the moon's orbit around Earth isn't a perfect circle. The moon's distance from Earth changes slightly from day to day. When the moon is closer to Earth, it appears to be larger. If an eclipse happens at this point, the moon can block out the entire Sun. This is called a total solar eclipse.

When the moon is farther away from Earth, it appears to be smaller than the Sun. If an eclipse happens at this point, you can still see a ring of sunlight around the edges of the moon. This is called an **annular** eclipse.

A third type of solar eclipse is called a partial eclipse. A partial eclipse happens when the moon blocks only a part of the Sun. During a partial eclipse, you can see a sliver of Sun to one side of the moon.

A solar eclipse happens when the moon blocks sunlight from reaching Earth.

This is a total solar eclipse. The moon has blocked the entire Sun.

Viewing a Solar Eclipse

Looking directly at a solar eclipse can damage your eyes forever. It is best to watch a solar eclipse on TV or to use special sunglasses. It is also easy to build a "pinhole camera" to watch the eclipse safely. Make a small hole in a piece of paper. Hold a second piece of paper 3 feet (1 meter) away. Sunlight will go through the hole and an image of the Sun will appear on the second piece of paper. As the moon moves across the Sun, a shadow will move across the circle of light on the second piece of paper.

A pinhole camera is a safe way to watch an eclipse.

eclipse—when one object in space blocks light and keeps it from shining on another object in space

annular—ring-shaped

11

Lunar eclipses are about as rare as solar eclipses. However, lunar eclipses can last longer. They can be seen from half of Earth. A total lunar eclipse happens when Earth blocks all sunlight from reaching the moon. The moon can lie entirely within the Earth's shadow for up to an hour. This is because Earth's shadow is so large relative to the moon.

A lunar eclipse happens when Earth blocks sunlight from reaching the moon.

AMAZING FACT

It is safe to look directly at a lunar eclipse, since there is no sunlight present to harm your eyes.

The moon appears red during a lunar eclipse. As light from the Sun passes around Earth, our atmosphere filters out the blue light. Only red and orange light is left behind to shine on to the moon's surface.

Before modern science was able to explain solar and lunar eclipses, people around the world created their own explanations. The Vikings thought eclipses happened when a wolf ate the Sun or moon. The ancient Vietnamese had a similar theory, but blamed it on a frog or toad. Korean and Hindu people believed that eclipses happened when someone tried to steal the Sun or moon. In parts of West Africa, people believed the Sun and moon were fighting. They viewed an eclipse as a time to make peace.

lunar—having to do with the moon

SOLAR WIND

The Sun releases a constant stream of particles, such as protons and electrons. This stream of particles is known as the solar wind. This isn't a wind like the winds we experience on Earth. The solar wind is caused by the intense heat of the Sun.

Most hot particles stay within the Sun. This is because the Sun, like Earth, has gravity. Gravity is the force that keeps people, animals, furniture, and everything else from floating off Earth's surface. The Sun's gravity also keeps most particles from floating away.

On both the Sun and Earth, objects have to move very fast to escape gravity. On Earth, we've launched rockets and spaceships that escape Earth's gravity and reach space. Those rockets and spaceships have to travel very fast. The same is true on the Sun. The particles that escape become the solar wind.

As the solar wind blows through our solar system, some of its particles hit Earth. The particles get caught in the magnetic field that wraps around our planet. This magnetic field connects to Earth in two different places: the North Pole and the South Pole.

When the solar wind particles hit the magnetic field, the particles move toward the North Pole and South Pole. The particles eventually reach the top of Earth's **atmosphere**. There, they collide with gas particles in the atmosphere. This can create beautiful colored lights in the sky. Near the North Pole, we call these lights the aurora borealis, or northern lights. Near the South Pole, they are the aurora australis, or southern lights.

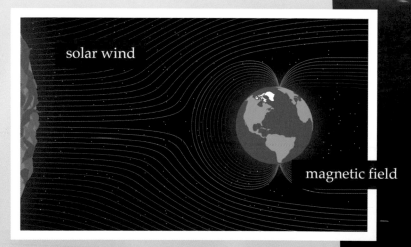

The magnetic field around Earth protects it from solar winds.

However, most of the solar wind passes by Earth. It stops at a distance about 90 times as far as the distance between the Sun and Earth. Where the solar wind stops, its particles form a huge bubble surrounding our Sun and all the planets. This bubble is called the **heliopause**. This marks the edge of our solar system. Beyond that is **interstellar** space.

AMAZING FACT

Imagine that you could take a spaceship out to the heliopause. From that distance, if you looked back at our Sun, it would look tiny. It would appear to be a small white dot, like any other star in the sky.

atmosphere—the layer of gases that surrounds Earth

heliopause—the outer edge of our solar system, where the solar wind stops

interstellar—between the stars

SOLAR FLARES AND EJECTIONS

We've already learned about how small particles leaving the Sun make up the solar wind. Larger bursts of particles that leave the Sun are called solar **flares** or solar **ejections**. Both flares and ejections contain particles that have an electric charge. This means they can affect magnetic fields.

Solar flares are smaller bursts than solar ejections. Flares can reach the upper atmosphere of Earth. They are labeled differently depending on how strong they are. The labels are A, B, C, M, and X. A-class, B-class, and C-class flares are too weak to affect the Earth. M-class and X-class flares are the strongest.

Solar ejections are stronger than solar flares. Solar ejections can interfere with activity all the way down on the ground. It can take one to three days for a solar ejection to reach the Earth after it's released from the Sun. Billions of tons of particles can be released with a solar ejection. They move at an average speed of 375 miles (600 km) per second.

solar flare

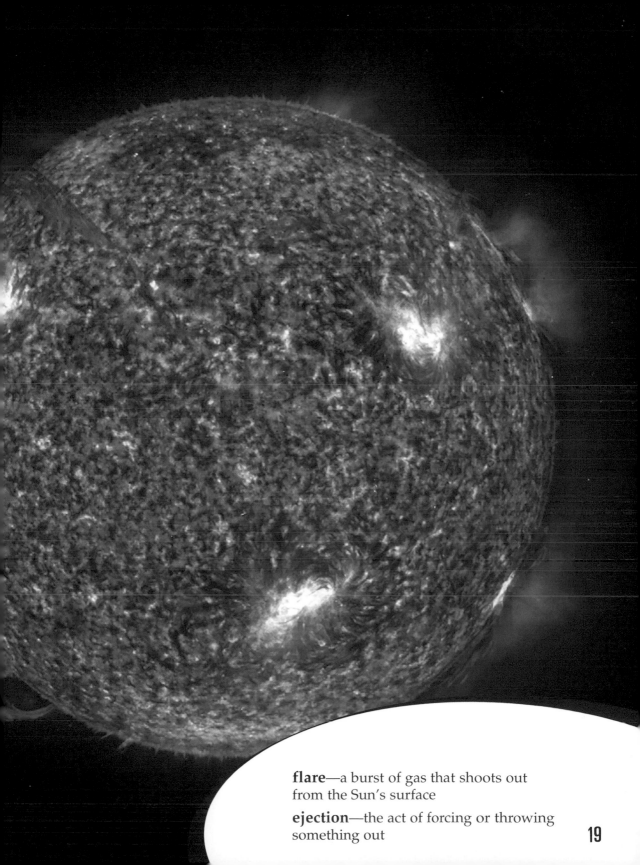

flare—a burst of gas that shoots out from the Sun's surface

ejection—the act of forcing or throwing something out

AMAZING FACT

In 1859 two British astronomers saw an intense flash of light on the Sun. Two minutes later, the Kew Observatory in London measured a change in the Earth's magnetic field. This was the first time people connected activity on the Sun to activity on Earth. At the time, the term "solar flare" did not yet exist.

Humans have put many machines into space. These include satellites and other spacecraft. Spacecraft can be used for many purposes such as communications, monitoring weather, and studying the Sun and other planets.

Both solar flares and solar ejections can cause problems if they pass too close to spacecraft. The electric charge of solar flares and ejections can keep spacecraft from running correctly. When solar flares or ejections affect satellites, TV and radio broadcasts might be affected. Our cell phones might stop working for a moment. Or our GPS devices that help us get directions could be wrong.

Solar flares can affect satellites orbiting Earth.

Solar flares are too weak to affect activities on the ground. However, solar ejections can. They can't harm people, but they can interrupt electronics and our electric power. One of the biggest events caused by a solar ejection happened in Canada in 1989. A huge solar ejection traveled toward Earth at 1 million miles (1.6 million km) per hour. When it reached Earth, it caused a magnetic "storm." Although people didn't feel it, it caused electrical currents to run underground in North America. This current knocked out power in Quebec. Millions of people were without power for 12 hours.

Huge eruptions from the Sun are called coronal mass ejections.

GREEN FLASH

Imagine you are standing on a beach at sunset. The Sun is dropping below the **horizon**. You glance at the sky and see a flash of green light at the top edge of the Sun. You may think this light is only in your imagination. But it's not! It's a phenomenon known as the green flash.

The green flash is seen at sunset or sunrise, when the Sun is low on the horizon. It's hard to see the horizon when there are buildings and trees around. So the green flash is most often seen over an ocean, desert, or field.

The cause of the green flash is Earth's atmosphere. The gases in the atmosphere cause light to bend as it passes through. This effect is stronger the closer you get to the horizon. This is why the green flash is usually observed when only a tiny bit of the Sun is visible over the horizon.

horizon—the line where the sky and Earth or sea seem to meet

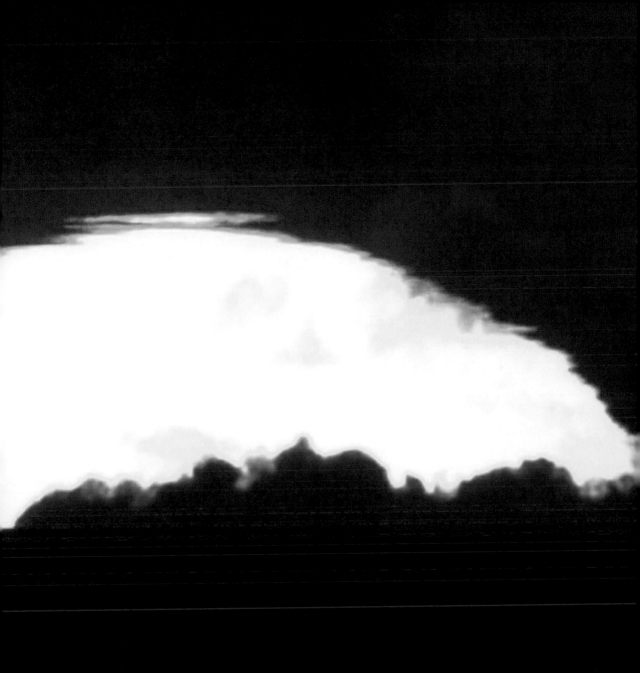

But why does the atmosphere cause the light to flash green? To understand this, you have to understand how light works. White light is made up of every color visible to humans. Each color travels through air in a slightly different way. Because each color of light moves differently, each color responds differently to bending.

The Earth's atmosphere breaks sunlight into individual colors, just like a prism. Each color bends in a different way. Blue light bends more strongly than red light. As the sun dips below the horizon the colors

The blue flash is even rarer than the green flash.

disappear one at a time, starting with the ones that bend least. When conditions are just right, all colors except green disappear and so we see a green flash. Some people have reported seeing a blue flash, but this is truly rare.

The Sun isn't the only object in the sky that can produce a green flash. A green flash can also be seen around the moon, other planets, and even very bright stars. In all cases, the green flash is visible only when the object is close to the horizon. It's always hard to spot. The green flash lasts for only a few seconds at most.

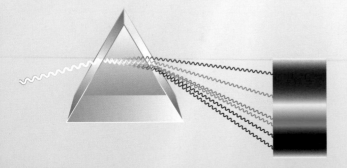

Light splits into different colors when it passes through Earth's atmosphere. The colors bend in different ways. Green shows up the strongest close to the horizon, so we see a green flash.

It is very difficult to photograph a green flash. The location and atmospheric conditions have to be exactly right.

SUN DOGS

High in the atmosphere, where it's very cold, water in the air can form ice crystals. These ice crystals are always shaped like **hexagons**. As light passes through them, they bend the light in different directions.

If these ice crystals have their flat sides toward the ground, they can bend sunlight in different ways. Sometimes they cause one or two bright spots to appear on either side of the Sun. Those bright spots can sometimes be bright enough to look like second or third suns. At other times, the ice crystals can create rainbows near the Sun. These bright spots and rainbows are called "sun dogs."

No one is sure where the term "sun dog" comes from. The scientific name for a sun dog is a **parhelion**. This word comes from the ancient Greek words meaning "beside the Sun."

Another phenomenon related to sun dogs is called the 22 degree halo. This is a ring of light that appears to circle the Sun. It is caused by sunlight passing through ice crystals that face in many different directions in the air.

hexagon—a flat shape with six equal sides

parhelion—the scientific name for a sun dog, occurring when ice crystals in the sky bend sunlight to make rainbows or bright lights appear

In recent years, the rise in shared videos online has revealed a new phenomenon related to sun dogs. Some videos seem to show sun dogs jumping around. In one video, a sun dog is hidden behind a cloud. Light shines one direction to create the sun dog. Then when the light switches direction, the bright spot appears to move.

No one is sure what causes these "jumping" sun dogs. Some scientists think the electric field from lightning in the cloud makes the ice crystals move. When the crystals move, the sun dog moves. But this is just a **hypothesis**. No one is sure what causes this phenomenon.

Jumping sun dogs are just one example of the many mysteries the Sun still holds for us. These mysteries will continue to be studied by scientists around the world. There is still much for us to learn and understand about our Sun.

hypothesis—a prediction that can be tested about how a scientific investigation will turn out

Glossary

annular (AN-yuh-ler)—ring-shaped

astronomer (as-TRON-uh-mer)—a scientist who studies stars, planets, and other objects in space

atmosphere (AT-muhss-feer)—the layer of gases that surrounds Earth

axis (AK-sis)—an imaginary line around which something rotates

eclipse (ih-KLIPS)—when one object in space blocks light and keeps it from shining on another object in space

ejection (ih-JEK-shun)—the act of forcing or throwing something out

flare (FLAIR)—a burst of gas that shoots out from the Sun's surface

heliopause (HEE-lee-uh-pawz)—the outer edge of our solar system, where the solar wind stops

hexagon (HEK-suh-gahn)—a flat shape with six equal sides

horizon (huh-RYE-zuhn)—the line where the sky and Earth or sea seem to meet

hypothesis (hye-POTH-uh-sis)—a prediction that can be tested about how a scientific investigation will turn out

interstellar (in-ter-STEL-er)—between the stars

lunar (LOO-ner)—having to do with the moon

parhelion (pahr-HEE-lee-uhn)—the scientific name for a sun dog, occurring when ice crystals in the sky bend sunlight to make rainbows or bright lights appear

particle (PAR-ti-kuhl)—a very tiny piece of an object

phenomena (fe-NOM-uh-nuh)—very unusual or remarkable events

solar (SOH-ler)—having to do with the Sun

telescope (TEL-uh-skohp)—an instrument made of lenses and mirrors that is used to view distant objects

Read More

Berne, Emma Carlson. *Totally Wacky Facts About Planets and Stars.* Mind Benders. North Mankato, Minn.: Capstone Press, 2016.

Hunter, Nick. *Northern Lights.* The Night Sky: and Other Amazing Sights. Chicago: Capstone Heinmann Library, 2013.

Reilly, Carmel. *The Sun.* Sky Watching. New York: Marshall Cavendish Benchmark, 2012.

Rockett, Paul. *70 Thousand Million, Million, Million Stars in Space.* The Big Countdown. Chicago: Capstone Raintree, 2016.

Internet Sites

FactHound offers a safe, fun way to find Internet sites related to this book. All of the sites on FactHound have been researched by our staff.

Here's all you do:

Visit *www.facthound.com*

Type in this code: 9781515707783

 Check out projects, games and lots more at
www.capstonekids.com

Critical Thinking Using the Common Core

1. How would you watch a solar eclipse safely?
   [Key Ideas and Details]

2. Describe the conditions that can cause sun dogs to appear.
   [Craft and Structure]

3. What is solar wind? How do you think solar wind might affect life on Earth if Earth's magnetic field was not there to protect us? [Integration of Knowledge and Ideas]

Index